Self-Organization In 8 Weeks

Your Ultimate Guide To A More Organized And Productive Life

Table of Contents

Introduction

This book contains proven steps and strategies on how to organize yourself and your life in general within eight short weeks.

If you want to be successful in life, you need to organize your life so you can get more things done in the shortest time possible. Organization is one of the keys to success. You may think that 24 hours is not enough to finish all the things that you need to do, but this is not true. A lot of busy people are successful in what they do and still have enough time for their personal life. This means they must be doing something right with their time. Organizing is a lot more than de-cluttering and making a to-do list. It takes a lot of effort on your part, but the eventual rewards are worth it.

This book gives you some useful tips and information about self-organization which includes time optimization, effective planning, increasing productivity, eliminating distractions, and a lot more. You will also be given challenges for each week to help you become more organized and permanently change your ways for the better.

Benefits Of Self-Organization

The term self-organization may seem misleading because it implies that it happens on its own, without any prompting. In reality, achieving self-organization actually requires a conscious effort on your part.

Self-organization simply means organizing your mind, actions, time, home, relationships, work, and your life in general. It is important to keep yourself organized if you want to be successful in life.

To understand self-organization better, you need to understand the three factors that make up the 'Triangle of Self-organization." This includes *goals, rules, and pressure.* The goals are accomplishments you want in the future. The rules are the dos and don'ts you need to follow – like the tips provided in this book. These will guide you and keep you on a straight path toward achieving your goals.

Finally, pressure is the factor that keeps you going. This can be your motivation to follow the rules and to achieve your goals. These three factors make up self-organization, and you will learn more about them throughout this book.

The motivation behind self-organization can be the benefits you get from it. The goals and the pressure sometimes overlap. For example, your main goal for working hard, which is to provide a comfortable life for your family, can also be the pressure or motivation that keeps you going.

Here are some other benefits of self-organization that can serve as your goal or pressure depending on how you look at it.

4

Less stress

De-stressing is one of the main reasons people decide to practice self-organization. Being organized lowers your stress level in many different ways.

For example, if you organize your office and get rid of clutter, you can easily find the things you need, which means less stress. If you clear your mind from negative and unnecessary thoughts, you will no longer be stressed because you can think clearly. If you make careful plans, you will know what steps to take, which makes you feel less rattled and overwhelmed no matter how huge the task is.

Reducing your stress level also improves your health because stress weakens your immune system. It also makes your life happier. Lowering your stress level is important, and organizing yourself and your life in general is a good way to achieve that.

More free time

Organizing yourself does not mean you must fill your daily schedule with only urgent tasks that have consequences if you do not complete them. Self-organization also includes having enough free time to pursue the activities you want to do, like your hobbies or spending time with your family.

Being organized means accomplishing the things you need to do as soon as possible, so you have enough time to do what you want afterwards. If you finish all your tasks and chores, you can at least enjoy your free time better because you do not have to worry about deadlines or an unfinished job. Having enough time to spend with your family will surely improve your relationship with them and make your personal life more satisfying.

Large tasks seem easier to handle

If you are well-organized and you plan your actions carefully, you will not feel as overwhelmed with large tasks and difficult chores you need to finish. Designing and scheduling your tasks gives you a sense of control. One aspect of careful planning, which you learn more about later, is breaking down a big task into smaller, more manageable tasks. This is something that self-organization encourages you to do. Tasks become easier to handle if they are clearly defined and you understand what needs to be done to take the task off your to-do list.

Fewer mistakes

Another important benefit of self-organization is making fewer mistakes. You will commit fewer mistakes because no small details go unnoticed. For instance, if you are writing a research paper and your notes are in complete disarray, you might miss some important details that should be in your paper. Because of this, you might receive a low grade for writing an incomplete research paper. If you have fewer mistakes because your work is organized and carefully planned, you do not have to worry about low marks or revisions that mean extra time and effort.

Get more things done

Self-organization also helps you get more done in the shortest time possible. If you are organized, your productivity significantly increases. At work, you probably have a lot of tasks to finish within the day.

If you organize your tasks by writing them down from most to the least important, or breaking large tasks into smaller tasks, you can finish more in a short span of time. Moreover, when you get more done, it means you have more time to relax while your coworkers continue trying to beat the deadline. Your boss will also be happy with your efficiency.

Inspire others

Your kids will see you as someone who works hard but still has plenty of time for family, friends, and hobbies. They look up to you as a role model and they eventually adopt your best practices as their own. You can also be a source of inspiration for your coworkers. Your hard work can help them recognize that nothing is impossible if you put your mind to it and if you keep your life organized.

Keep a journal for this 8-week challenge

The next few chapters provide the tips and challenges to help you organize yourself and change your life for the better within eight weeks. Each chapter has specific challenges you need to accomplish. You are also encouraged to keep track of your progress, so you know if you are moving toward your goals. This also lets you know what kind of changes you have made in your life during the 8-week period.

You should write down the challenges you need to finish for each week based on the following chapters, and write down problems you have encountered and the solutions you have come up with to solve them. Do not forget to write the amount of time you spent on the challenges where time monitoring is applicable. You can also write your long-term and short-term goals, which serve as your master list. This will be your guide and motivation for taking on this 8-week challenge. It is also important to write daily tasks and your daily schedule, and check them off until you have completed everything

By writing down your long-term and short-term goals, your weekly challenges, and your daily tasks and schedule, you know if you are on the right track to achieve ultimate self-organization. Keep in mind that the challenges are not meant for that specific week only. The challenges in this book are intended for you to form habits that promote self-organization and should be practiced beyond this 8-week self-organization challenge.

Week 1—Time Optimization

Time is of the essence for people who have busy schedules. Every second counts with everything needing completion, so it is important to know how to optimize your time for maximum self-organization. It is essential to use your time wisely, so you can accomplish all the tasks you set out to do.

Optimizing your time not only means using every waking hour to finish your work and chores. It also means knowing how to better manage your time to allow you to pursue hobbies and interests and spend more time with family and friends.

Time optimization does not just focus on tangible, measurable goals. Rather, it also focuses on the quality of experiences you have. The whole point of living is not to accomplish tasks but to experience and enjoy every moment. You can only enjoy your experiences if you know how to optimize your time. Here are some lifestyle changes you can make to better optimize your time.

Wake up early

Have you ever heard of the saying, "The early bird gets the worm?" This is true because those who wake up early accomplish more and enjoy their lives more. How is that possible, when sleeping in gives you such a good feeling? If you wake up early, you can finish your tasks earlier, which gives you more free time to do things you love to do. You can also enjoy waking up to a quiet morning with only the sound of the birds chirping and the sun just about to appear on the horizon. This alone can help you start your day right. You will also have the feeling that you have already accomplished a lot and are ahead of schedule, while you see everyone else with sleep still in their eyes.

Automate

Another useful tip to better optimize your time is to automate several aspects of your life. Automation was originally used in an industrial context where factories used machineries and automatic processes to improve productivity. Today, automation is used in other areas, as well. There is office automation in which all the processes in the office are connected to one system for higher productivity. Automation is also used at home when you decide to prewire your home so all the electrical systems – alarm, lighting, thermostat, security camera, and audio systems – can be controlled using one computer or remote control. If your home is automated, your life will be easier because you do not have to turn on or off electrical fixtures one at a time. It also allows you to control your house no matter where you are. Automation is a big help when you go on vacation for several days because you can set a timer for your thermostat and lighting, so the house warms upon your return and the lights turn on and off at the scheduled times even while you are gone.

Another way to optimize your time using automation is to enroll in automatic payments. You can enroll all your utility bills like electric, water, gas, telephone, and cable bills, so they are automatically deducted from your bank account on the due date. You can also enroll your credit cards to prevent you from having late payments, which can affect your credit score. If you decide to automate your bill payments, make sure your bank account always has enough money to pay for all the bills when the due dates arrive.

Streamline

There are millions of ways to accomplish one task, and you need to find the easiest one for you. Streamlining your tasks helps you finish them quickly. However, this does not mean you have to skip steps or compromise the quality of your output. Still aim for high quality output, but you need to find the easiest way to achieve this output.

For example, if you need to send emails with the same content to all your coworkers, you do not have to re-type the email for each person. Instead, you can cc or "carbon copy" the email to all the intended recipients, sending the email to everyone at once. Before you start a task, first find the best way to accomplish it. This way, you can finish more tasks in the shortest time possible with the least effort.

Use a smart phone

This gadget is called a smart phone because it can do a lot of things for you. Smart phones have many features that can make your life easier, such as an alarm clock, organizer, calendar, and reminders. These are already installed in your phone when you buy it, so you can use them right away. There are also applications you can download, such as Evernote, that allow you to save files in different formats, meaning you can access them anywhere you go and no matter what device you are using. These features in your smart phone also help you optimize your time, which can lead you to self-organization.

Aside from organization tools, a smart phone can also be used as a camera, music player, video and voice recorder, and a navigation system. When you go out and you need all these things, you do not need to waste time searching for them one-by-one. Just make sure you use your smart phone wisely because it can sometimes be a source of distraction.

Hire someone or delegate

Another tip for time optimization is to hire someone to do the task for you or to delegate. By letting someone else do it for you, you have more time to do the most important tasks on your list. Just remember that this is only for tasks that are not considered your responsibilities or tasks that you do because no one else is doing them. For example, if you have a business and if business is growing, you should consider hiring a bookkeeper who can help manage your accounts, so you can focus your attention on the core functions of your business. When cleaning the house, you can delegate some tasks to your children, like cleaning their own rooms and other small tasks.

Week 1 tasks

Here is a list of tasks for Week 1 to help you practice time optimization and make it a part of your habit and lifestyle.

1. Wake up earlier than usual. If you usually wake up at 6am and go to work at 7am, try to get up at 5:30am on the first and second day. On the third day and fourth day, wake up at

5am. You can wake up even earlier at 4:30am on the last three days of Week 1 and the days to follow until it become a permanent part of your routine. You can go out for a morning jog or cook meals your family can eat throughout the day.

2. Enroll your utility bills and credit card bills in an automated payment system. Keep in mind: 1) your bank account should have enough money to cover all the payments, and 2) schedule your payments a couple of business days before the due date, so you have enough time to fix any problem that may arise

3. Find crock pot recipes and slow cook your meals. Crock pots cook your meals slowly and allow you to do other things while the food is cooking.

4. Utilize the features in your smart phone. Input your schedule in the organizer, use the alarm to accomplish task #1, and use the reminder feature to help you remember deadlines, appointments, and other important events.

5. Organize a general clean up in your house. Assign yourself the living room, kitchen, and master bedroom. Assign your children their own bedrooms. Delegate several small tasks like taking out the trash, watering the plants, feeding the pets, and washing the dishes.

6. Hire someone to mow your lawn or clean your attic and basement.

In your journal

Write down the tasks above and put a check mark beside each task you accomplish. Include the details such as the amount of time spent, the people who helped you, problems you encountered, solutions to these problems, and other tasks relevant to time optimization but not included in the list of tasks for Week 1.

Week 2—Increase Productivity

Almost all people who have a job have a busy schedule. Sometimes, the number of hours they need to stay at the office goes beyond the regular 8 to 9 hours a day. This is why a lot of people work overtime by adding one or more hours per day several times a week, working on weekends, or bringing their work at home. Although it may be true that there are too many tasks to accomplish in one day, it is also highly possible that you are not being efficient, which means you are not using your time wisely.

If you want to be productive and efficient, you need careful planning, effective time management, and focused efforts. It can be a challenge to become productive at home and at work because of all the things that can distract you. When the day ends, you are often not satisfied with how you spent your day and you regret that you were unable to accomplish everything. You can stop feeling this way if you use the following tips to improve your productivity.

Manage your to-do list

It is a given that you need to have a master list where you can write everything that needs to be done for the day. This makes it easier for you to track the tasks. However, it is not enough to have a to-do list. It is also important to manage your to-do list properly.

For example, you should rank your tasks according to level or urgency or importance. Those that are urgent and important should be at the top of your list, followed by important but not so urgent, and urgent but not so important. You also need to evaluate your list. Make sure that all the tasks included there are things you really need to do. If there are tasks you can drop from your list, you should do so to make your list more focused on what matters. Sometimes, people get too overwhelmed with their long list of things to do because they include unnecessary tasks.

Another tip to better manage your to-do list is to stop adding tasks once you have finished all the tasks. You should give yourself enough time to rest, so you can refresh your mind and recharge your body for the next day's new set of tasks.

Focus on one task at a time

Keep your mind focused on the task at hand and stop yourself from thinking about the other tasks you still need to do. This only makes you feel overwhelmed. When you find yourself thinking about another task while working on one already, remind yourself there is time for that task once you finish what you are currently doing.

Another way to focus on the task at hand is to avoid multi-tasking. Some people view multi-tasking as the solution to their problem. They think that being able to multi-task makes them more productive. While you may be able to finish several tasks within a shorter time frame, the quality of your work will surely be affected. It is more difficult to think if your mind is constantly shifting from one task to another. You may end up with poor quality output or several unfinished tasks.

Know your work habits

You need to know your work habits, so you can schedule your day around it. For example, if you are the type of person who tires of doing the same thing for several hours straight, you should consider switching between assignments to give yourself more variety and to keep it interesting. This is not the same as multitasking because you are doing different things one at a time. For example, for the first two hours, you can work on research. You can spend the next two hours replying to emails. Afterward, look into the material your boss gave you. You can then go back to doing the first task. However, if you are the type who prefers to finish one task before moving on to another, then you should not follow this work habit.

You should also identify your peak hours or the hours when you feel the most alert and energetic. Schedule complicated tasks and tasks that require a lot of thinking during your peak hours. For instance, if you think you can be most productive early in the morning because this is the time when your mind is still clear and alert, schedule writing that report or drafting your proposal at this time. If you know your energy starts to wane after lunch, then you should schedule low-value tasks during that time, like de-cluttering your office or reading emails.

Beat laziness and procrastination

Procrastination and laziness keep you from being productive. Procrastination is when you put off tasks you need to do and do easier, low-value tasks instead that do not really reduce your workload. Laziness is the state-of-mind when you simply do not want to work. The key here is to get started and take that first step. The first step is usually the most difficult part of the task, but once you start, you find the momentum to keep you going.

Another way to beat procrastination and laziness is to remind yourself of your goals and motivation. Remind yourself why it is important to finish the task right away and of the consequences for failing to complete it.

Time yourself

Time yourself when doing tasks to ensure you can finish everything on your to-do list. Remember to set reasonable deadlines for each task. Otherwise, you will feel overwhelmed and frustrated because you cannot follow your overly strict schedule. When you work, set a timer to remind you that you should be wrapping up your work and moving on to the next task.

Week 2 tasks

1. Create a master list every day for the rest of the week that looks like the table below. Of course, you can add more tasks and tweak this, but the general format should look like this.

TIME	TASK	STATUS	NOTES
7AM-8AM	Attend meeting	Done	Discussed next month's budget
8AM-9AM	Start the report	Just started	Submit partial draft to manager by

			9AM
9AM-10AM	Reply to emails	Did not do yet	Reply only to important emails

2. Make sure all the tasks have the "Done" status at the end of the day. If not, specify the reason why you could not finish it on time. Be sure that the reason is valid and not just an excuse to get out of work.
3. As a challenge, do a general cleanup at home on Saturday, Day 7 of Week 2. You should include the following tasks:
   - ✓ Clean the master bedroom (organize the closet, change the bed linens, get rid of the clutter, vacuum the floor, wipe surfaces)
   - ✓ Clean the bathroom (clean the bathtub, toilet, sink, and flooring; clear the cabinets and get rid of empty bottles and boxes; put fresh towels)
   - ✓ Clean the kitchen (wash the dishes, put the dishes in the dish rack, organize the pantry and cupboards, clean the kitchen appliances, clear the countertops, vacuum and mop the floor)
   - ✓ Clean the living room and dining room (get rid of clutter, wipe surfaces, vacuum upholstery and rugs, change drapes and curtains, vacuum the floor)
   - ✓ Let the other members of the household clean their own bedrooms and clutter
   - ✓ Delegate tasks to each member of the household
4. Buy a timer you can use to monitor yourself while working.

5. Identify your peak and off-peak hours. Group all the complicated tasks and tasks that require a lot of effort, and complete them during your peak hours. This includes writing a report, bookkeeping, and research. Group all low-value tasks, and finish them during your off peak hours. This may include de-cluttering your office, responding to emails, making a phone call, and so on.

In your journal

Be sure to write your daily to-do list in your journal and monitor your progress every hour. Your daily to-do list may change every day but there are tasks that you have to do every day. For the third challenge, write a more-detailed list that includes all other small tasks not included in the list above. Write your peak and off-peak hours, group your tasks according to difficulty, and decide when you should do them.

Week 3—Plan Effectively

Success does not happen spontaneously. You must carefully plan ahead of time, so you can be better prepared when it comes to doing the tasks that lead to your success. Effective planning is one aspect of self-organization. You need to know how to plan ahead, especially on tasks that are complicated, to keep you focused and to prevent procrastination.

Effective planning gives you direction. You plan your tasks carefully because you want to ensure your tasks are done properly. It also minimizes risks, uncertainties and wasteful activities. With planning, you use your time the best way possible. If you plan your day, you give yourself more control over the future. Sometimes, things do not go according to plan, but if you practice effective planning, you likely have a plan B or C just in case.

Tips for effective planning are as follows:

Define your goals

The first step to effective planning is to clearly define your goals. The ultimate goal for your daily planning is to finish all the tasks for the day by the end of the work day. Your specific tasks also have their own corresponding goals. For example, if your task is to write a monthly report, the goal would be to submit the report to your boss by 10 am. Using your journal, you can put your tasks and goals into writing, which helps you remember what you need to accomplish.

List the tasks you need to do in order to achieve your goal

Going back to the previous example, if your goal is to submit the report by 10 am, outline everything you need to do to achieve this goal. For example, you may need to research on a specific topic for your report, get an important document from your supervisor, make a phone call to confirm a specific detail, and so on. Be sure you order them logically, with the first step at the top of your list and the last step at the bottom. You should also allot a specific timeframe for the completion of each task. If you list all the tasks that need to be done, you have a more systematic approach to help you reach your goal faster.

Determine whether you need help or not

The next step is to define your responsibilities or the specific tasks you are responsible for. If the task is solely your responsibility, you can skip this step altogether. However, if it requires the help of other people, it is important that your and their roles are clearly defined, so everyone knows what is expected of them. This also prevents multiple people completing the same task twice. If you need the help of other people to accomplish the task, they need to know their roles and how much time they should spend on each task. It is better if you consult them first before you delegate tasks and make assignments, especially if you are not the team leader. Otherwise, they may feel you are bossing them around.

Create a timeline

Once you have clarified the goal, the tasks, the amount of time needed for each task, and the key players in completing the different tasks, you now need to create a timeline or schedule flow you and your team can follow. For example, you can schedule the major task on a specific day and the smaller tasks at specific hours of the day. If it is a project that requires several days or weeks to be accomplished, you should plan the schedule and explain the timeline to your team carefully to ensure you move toward your goal every day. You can create milestones in your timeline, like submitting the first draft or gathering all important information on the first day or dividing the project among several major parts. Make a copy of this timeline and give one to each team member.

Evaluate your performance regularly

Effective planning also involves evaluation of your performance to know if you are on the right track. This is especially important if you are working on a large project. Regular evaluation allows you to correct mistakes early on to prevent you from revising issues later on. This is also important if you are working with a team. Regular evaluation ensures that everyone is doing their job properly and everyone is working on schedule. If you are working alone, you should take a few minutes to evaluate your progress and make any necessary adjustments. You can evaluate after every significant milestone or after every hour or so. It depends on what works best for you and the task.

Review your planning process

Once you have completed the project, you should review the planning methodology you used to see whether it was effective or not. Keep in mind that different projects may require different planning methods, and you need to know what kind works for the specific task or goal you are working on. One sign that the planning process is successful is when you were able to complete the project on time with high quality. Another sign is if the members of your team were able to complete their work properly without any trouble.

Week 3 tasks

1. Create a 7-day meal plan for your family. Creating a meal plan at the start of the week allows you to prepare healthy meals that provide all the nutrients your family needs. This also helps you stick to your budget more easily because you know how much you need to spend for each meal. If you have a special diet, like a clean or gluten-free diet, planning your meals in advance is even more beneficial. To plan a 7-day meal plan for your family, you need to include breakfast, morning snack, lunch, afternoon snack, and dinner. You can research for recipes online that adhere to the kind of diet your family follows. You can even find the nutritional information of each recipe and the number of calories for each meal. You need to take into consideration the number of people in your household and adjust the recipes accordingly.

2. List your weekly groceries. Once you have created your meal plan, you can now list all the groceries you need. Write the ingredients for each meal and the corresponding amount. Group similar grocery items together, like fresh produce, meat, dairy products and milk, packaged food, drinks, condiments, and so on. Schedule your shopping trip at the beginning of the week, on early Sunday morning, or Saturday afternoon for your next week's

groceries. You can even download the map of the grocery or supermarket, so you do not have to go through every aisle. If you have coupons, bring them with you to get discounts.

3. Plan your schedule every day before going to bed. If you want to have a good night sleep, you should consider planning your schedule before bedtime. Write down everything you need to do in your planner or journal and assign a schedule to each task.

In your journal

For Week 3, write down all the tasks you have planned and the steps you took for more effective planning. Do not forget to write down the amount of time you used to complete each task using effective planning. You can also compare doing the task before and after you used effective and systematic planning in terms of the time consumed and allotted budget.

Week 4—Identify And Eliminate Distractions

The world today is different from the world that our parents grew up in decades ago. Today, there are a lot of distractions that keep you from doing your job – from watching TV and browsing the internet to playing video games and checking your smart phone. Most of the time, these distractions are caused by electronic gadgets – the same gadgets that are supposed to streamline your tasks and make your life easier.

These electronic gadgets are not actually the problem. Rather, it is the way you use them that keeps you distracted from finishing your job. Some people spend hours browsing the internet for useless information or playing video games the whole day. Although there is nothing wrong with going online and checking your Facebook account or playing a game, you have to make sure you limit the amount of time you spend doing these activities. To give you further tips and advice for identifying and eliminating sources of distractions, read through the following paragraphs.

What are the common sources of distractions?

Identifying the main causes of your distraction is the first step to eliminating them. As mentioned earlier, electronic gadgets like TV, video games, internet, and smart phones are the most common causes of distractions. Aside from these, other sources of distractions include clutter in our home and office, low-value tasks you need to get out of the way, noises and racket caused by your children, an unclear mind, and so on. Once you have identified the main causes of your distraction, it will be easier for you to find a solution to your problem, so you can stop getting distracted, start improving self-organization, and start boosting your productivity.

Stay away from or turn off electronic gadgets

Stay away from your Xbox or Playstation, and do not turn on the TV. You can also turn off your smart phone or at least turn off the notifications if you need to receive messages or are waiting for an important phone call. By turning off your smart phone's notification, you prevent yourself from checking it constantly. You cannot simply turn off your computer if you are using it to work. What you can do instead is close all tabs you do not use and make you distracted and avoid sites like Facebook, Twitter, and others that you do not need for work. Your company may even block Facebook and other websites from your computer, because they want you to stay productive. Some people even choose to disconnect their computer from the internet to be sure they do not check their social media accounts while working.

Check your email only once or twice a day

Checking your email can also be a source of distraction. When your email is open right in front of you or when you always hear the notification from your cell phone from receiving an email, you are tempted to check the email. What you need to do is to schedule when you check your email. It could be once in the morning and once in the afternoon. Use these times to reply to and send important emails. When you schedule your email processing, you can

27

avoid wasting several minutes of every day checking your email all the time.

De-clutter

Another common source of distraction is clutter. If your office or home is cluttered, you will find it difficult to focus because you experience visual stress. Most people cannot work well in a cluttered space. You should clear your office desk before working and make sure your house is clear if you work at home. Regular de-cluttering is important, so you do not have to spend a lot of time and effort clearing your accumulated clutter. This is an important aspect of self-organization and will be discussed in detail in the next chapter.

Find a quiet place to work

To ensure that the noise and other outside stimuli do not distract you, consider finding a quiet place to work. This is easy if you have your own office. All you need to do is lock your door and hang a "do not disturb" sign. If you do not have your own office and work side-by-side coworkers, you can simply wear headphones to discourage conversation. It is difficult to avoid distractions at home. If you work at home, make sure you assign a space for your home office to allow you to work peacefully.

Complete easy tasks immediately

To get them out of the way and help your mind focus on more important tasks, you should consider completing the fast, easy tasks first. Once these are completed, your mind can focus on the more important tasks instead of always worrying about the minor ones, like taking out the trash, washing the dishes, replying to an email, and so on. Just remember not to dawdle too much on low-value tasks. It should only take a few minutes of your time, or you will have too little time left for more important tasks.

Schedule downtime

You also need to schedule downtime while working. For example, you can check your Facebook every hour for five minutes instead of checking it all the time. This is the same as scheduling your email processing for a couple of times per day. You can also check your smart phone every two hours or so. Be sure to stick to your downtime schedule. Otherwise, you end up procrastinating more.

Week 4 tasks

1. For one whole week, limit yourself to one hour of using electronic gadgets every day. For example, you can play video games on Sunday, check your Facebook and Twitter and other social media accounts on Monday, play games on your cell phone on Tuesday, browse your favorite websites on Wednesday, watch movies on Thursday, watch TV series on Friday, and chat with friends on Saturday. Set aside one hour every day for your electronic gadgets. You can tweak this challenge a little bit. For example, if you are not into playing video games, you can use that hour for something you prefer to do, like watching TV.

2. When writing a report or paper that requires online research, you should do your research all at once for an hour or so then disconnect your laptop from the internet. Write your paper or report without being connected to the

internet. You will see how much more you can accomplish when you do this.

In your journal

Jot down the times when you were distracted while working, and identify the source of distraction. Write down the solution that helped you get rid of the distraction. This way, you know what kinds of things distract you the most, and what you can do to keep your focus.

Week 5—Get Rid Of Clutter

Getting rid of clutter was discussed briefly in the previous chapter. This deserves a whole chapter because of its impact on self-organization. Some people accumulate stuff for a number of reasons. For one, they associate memories with their things, and do not understand that the memories will still be there even without the object. Some people are simply hoarders, which is a kind of psychological disorder in which they cannot help but hold on to everything they own – even things most people consider garbage. Others simply love buying new things, especially when there is a sale, because it makes them feel good. These scenarios require expert intervention, usually by a psychiatrist. However, if the main reason you have a lot of clutter is your lack of organization, then this is something that can be easily addressed.

The goal of de-cluttering is to free up enough space in your home and office by disposing of things you no longer need or want, making it easier for you to access what you need. Here are some tips to de-clutter your life.

Devise a system for de-cluttering

If you are going to de-clutter your home or office, you should devise a system that makes it easy for you to get rid of clutter. Finding the right place to begin can sometimes be difficult, especially if you have a big house or office to organize. One way to de-clutter your home is to do it one room at a time. This will prevent you from feeling overwhelmed. In your office, you can start with your desk, before moving on to your file cabinets and shelves.

Use the triage method

If you have so much stuff and have no idea how to organize it, you should use the triage method to help you de-clutter your home and office. The three categories in this method are Keep, Get Rid Of, and Not Sure. Once you have categorized your possessions, you can throw away all the things that belong in the last two categories. You are probably wondering why you would immediately throw away things in the Not Sure category when you are not yet sure whether you want to keep them or not. The very fact that you are contemplating on getting rid of those items means you do not truly need them. These are things that may have sentimental value but you no longer need or want, or they are damaged objects you have been planning to repair for awhile but have not done so. You can donate, give away, sell, or throw away the stuff in the last two categories.

Have plenty of storage units

To keep your house and office clutter-free, you should have plenty of storage units like shelves, cabinets, drawers, boxes, baskets, and so on. If your belongings have a home, it will be easier to find them. Putting them away in these storage units also keeps them out of view, which eases stress. Just remember to keep only the things you need and want in these storage units, and always keep the contents organized. You do not want to have all your clothes in a pile in the closet. Your clothes should be hung or folded neatly to make it easier to find the outfit you are looking for. The main purpose of having storage units is to give everything a home and to avoid accumulating more materials you do not need.

Stop accumulating stuff

Another way to free your house and office from clutter is to stop accumulating stuff. This happens when you buy things you do not need. Do not buy items just because they are on sale. You may think you are saving money because of the discount, but if the item just stays at the back of your closet collecting dust, then you are wasting your money and adding clutter to your life. Do not think that being a collector gives you an excuse to accumulate junk. You might say you are a shoe collector, so having thousands of pairs of shoes is okay. It is not okay if your collection takes up all the free space in your home. If you cannot give your items a proper home, you should limit your collection to an amount your home can accommodate without sacrificing living space.

There are also people who hang onto old possessions because of the sentimental value. As you grow older, you have more and more experiences and memories you want to remember, and if you are the type of person who keeps ticket stubs and dried rose petals in a shoe box, you are probably keeping a lot of stuff at home with sentimental value. Although there are some things you should keep, like your wedding gown or an old family cookbook that has been passed down for generations, you should consider getting rid of some of the stuff because it is truly just clutter. Some examples are your child's old baby clothes that have been collecting dust in the closet for years, your college textbooks, and an ugly dining room set you got from your parents who passed away many years ago. You should separate memories from objects to make it easier to de-clutter.

Clean and clear whenever you can

When you wake up in the morning, make your bed before doing other things. Fold all your clean clothes and put them in your closet right away. Purge your drawers and closet every month or so. This way, your house will remain clutter-free, which makes it easier for you to clean and organize.

Week 5 tasks

1. Organize your closet. To organize your closet, you have to follow some rules to let you know which clothes and accessories you should keep. Dispose of clothes you have not worn for more than a year, ill-fitting clothes, clothes that are no longer appropriate for your age, clothes that you have been meaning to repair but have not, and clothes that are torn or have holes in them. You should put seasonal clothes at the back or on top of your closet in boxes, like your thick jackets, fur-lined coats, and swimsuits.
2. Whenever you see clutter in your house or room, clear it away and put it where it belongs.
3. If you have a collection of books that has been taking up too much space in your house, you should organize it by keeping only the books you really like and donating the rest of them to your local library. You can also download e-books if you still want to have copies of them.

In your journal

Write down the parts of your house or office you organized and how long it took you to complete the task. Observe how your newly organized house and office affect your day-to-day life, and write your observations in your journal.

Week 6—Clear Your Mind

One of the things that keep people from achieving ultimate self-organization is a mind filled with worries, which prevents you from focusing on your tasks. If you clear your mind, it is easier for you to follow your schedule and accomplish the tasks you have assigned yourself. Whenever you feel like tearing your hair out because of all the thoughts going through your head, you should consider clearing your mind to help you think clearly and solve problems more easily. Here are some useful tips you can try.

Write your thoughts down

Many people resort to writing whenever they want to clear their heads. You can keep a diary or a journal for all your ideas and thoughts, like the one you have especially for this challenge. More often than not, writing down your thoughts and reading them afterwards allows you to see things in a different perspective, as if you are reading another person's thoughts. It allows you to look at your problem objectively and helps you find solution you might have otherwise missed. This form of writing does not require you to observe proper grammar or write in a specific style because you will be the only one who reads it.

Go for a jog

Sometimes, the best way to get rid of unwanted thoughts in your head is to run away from them, literally. Whenever you have one of those days when you feel like your mind is in shambles, go for a jog. The regular rhythm of your breathing and your feet touching the concrete clears your mind. The smell of fresh air, the beautiful sounds of the birds, and the amazing sights of nature are better for your mind than your stuffy office. This is the reason why some people go out for a walk whenever they have a problem.

Talk it out

Another way to clear your mind is to talk about your troubles with someone close to you. If something is bugging you, like a problem or dilemma, you should consider confiding in someone you trust. This will help you in the same way that writing down your thoughts can help clear your head. When you articulate the thoughts running in your head, you can understand more clearly and find the right solution to your problem. Talking it out with someone you trust can also help you solve your dilemma because you can ask for advice. More often than not, all you need is to air out your thoughts and have someone listen to you without judging.

Remind yourself of the things that matter

When in doubt or when in a middle of a decision-making dilemma, always remind yourself about the things that really matter to you. This includes your family, friends, safety, health, basic needs, and freedom. The things that matter the most can lead you to the right decision. When your mind starts to wander and worry about a lot of things, you need to remember the important things in your life. This will remind you that you should not be spending your mental energy on things that are not significant in your life.

Try meditation

Meditation is another great way to clear your mind. You do not need to be a hippie or a highly spiritual person to practice meditation, and meditation has a lot of benefits. For one, it helps de-clutter your mind of thoughts that are not important. It also helps improve your focus by increasing your conscious awareness. This is where you allow thoughts to enter your mind and acknowledge them but let them pass by. One very effective form of meditation is breathing. In fact, a lot of meditation exercises include breathing at the beginning and at the end. Breathing helps clear your mind and allows you to manage your emotions. When you are angry, you should try breathing deeply to calm down. This is also true when you are nervous.

Go to a quiet place

When you feel like a lot of thoughts are crowding your head, you should consider going to a quiet place to help you organize your thoughts. You will not be able to hear yourself think if you are in a noisy place. If you need to do some mind clearing and problem solving, you should find a quiet place where you can relax. Some people clear their head while taking a hot bath. The soothing aroma of your bubble bath and the relaxing hot water can help you organize your thoughts. You can also go to a park, sit on a bench, and watch your surroundings. Looking at other people sometimes helps you understand that other people probably have it worse than you, and this can help you release the negative thoughts running through your head. If you are near the beach, you can do your thinking by the water, which can make you feel that your problems are tiny compared to the vastness of the sea, and that, in the grand scheme of things, these problems do not matter.

Week 6 tasks

1. Try these activities to help clear your mind:
   a) Physical activities – five minutes. You can do this during your short break at the office. Instead of taking a cigarette break, you should use your short break to walk for five minutes and clear your head.
   b) Be grateful – four minutes. After clearing your head by doing a physical activity for five minutes, you should now focus on things you are grateful for to allow positive thoughts to enter your head. You may be feeling overwhelmed with all the tasks at work, but at least you have a job.
   c) Meditation – three minutes. You can also try meditation for three minutes to clear your head. You can do the breathing technique where you breathe deeply several times, or you can try visualization where you visualize positive images in your head.
   d) Enjoy silence – two minutes. While your mind is still clear, you should bask in the glory of the peacefulness that it brought. You should enjoy the silence while it lasts by closing your eyes and just enjoying being alive.
   e) Deep breathing – one minute. Before going back to work, you should breathe deeply to prepare yourself for the tasks ahead.

2. You should write down all the important things in your life and post it on your wall or somewhere you can easily see as a reminder of

why you are doing what you have to do. This helps put things in perspective whenever you are feeling stressed out from all your work.

In your journal

List the thoughts that run through your head every day. Check which among these thoughts occupy your mind the most. Ask yourself why you always think this particular thought and if there is something you can do to stop yourself from worrying about it.

Week 7—Simplify Your Relationships

Another useful tip for ultimate self-organization is simplifying your relationships. Your relationships can also create chaos in your life that can affect not only your personal life but also your work life. Complicated relationships make you feel stressed out, which affects your life in a negative way. This is why you need to simplify your relationships in order to organize your life.

You need to simplify your relationships with the different people in your life like your partner, children, parents, siblings, friends, and coworkers. The tips provided in this chapter apply to all types of relationships. Here are some guidelines for simplifying your relationships.

End bad relationships

If you are in a toxic relationship with your partner, and it does nothing but give you heartaches and headaches, you should consider ending the relationship. Before ending it though, you need to exhaust all possible solutions for saving your relationship, especially if you are married. You have to consider all the consequences involved in ending your relationship. If you think the relationship really has to end and that it is the best decision for all the parties involved, then you should end it.

This tip also applies to your relationship with friends. There are those so-called friends who do not act like your friends at all. These are the people who gossip about you, criticize your every move, want to see you fail, and keep you from growing as an individual. You should end your friendship if it does nothing but cause you pain. You do not have to be rude when ending relationships. There is no need to say negative things about the other person or to broadcast it to all the people you know on Facebook. Just do it as privately and nicely as you can to avoid causing pain to the person who was once part of your life.

Learn how to say 'no'

Another way to simplify your relationship is to learn to say "no." Sometimes, you find yourself in social situations you do not care for because you just do know how to say no to a friend. If a friend asks you to go to a bar or party, but you do not feel like it because you are tired and would rather stay at home reading a book, you should politely decline. If a friend asks you to drive him to the airport but you have a lot of work to finish, you should find the courage to say no. Nothing terrible will happen if you utter this two-letter word. Your friend may be disappointed at first but if he is your true friend, he will get over it. Being agreeable all the time complicates your relationships because you are doing things you do not really like. You will only end up feeling resentful toward your friends even though they do not have any intentions of hurting you.

Do not cause drama

Although it is important to be assertive by saying no, you should also avoid being too aggressive and causing unnecessary drama. If it is not necessary to be assertive, you should just keep quiet and let the situation pass. For example, if you are eating in a restaurant and the server forgot to bring you a fork, you should call the attention of someone and simply ask for a fork. Do not bite the server's head off just because you do not have a fork. This is also true in personal relationships. If your roommate drank all your milk because he honestly thought it was his, you should just let it pass, especially if it happened just once. There are situations you should just let go to avoid complications.

Spend more time alone

Relationships are naturally complicated, but there are ways to make them less complicated. This is why sometimes, it is best to spend time by yourself. For example, when going on a vacation, you should consider going solo, which allows you to do the things you want and fully experience the trip without having to appease someone. If you have just broken up with your ex, do not enter another relationship right away. You should consider staying single for awhile to avoid complications. However, this tip does not mean you should not get married or find a partner. This just means there is nothing wrong with being single and doing things alone. You should enjoy your single life while it lasts.

Spend less time on Facebook

Sometimes, social networking sites like Facebook can cause complications in your relationships. For example, when you post a status on your Facebook page, one friend may think you are referring to her when, in fact, you are referring to yourself. This can cause misunderstanding between you and your friend. There are also many people who pretend to be someone else online. This may annoy you because you know the person is just pretending. To avoid these unnecessary negative feelings and thoughts, spend less time on Facebook and more time in person.

Week 7 tasks

1. Delete some of the contacts in your phonebook. Delete the numbers of people you have not contacted in years and those who you do not even remember anymore. If you recently broke up with your ex and still have his or her number, you should also delete the number to reduce the urge to call.
2. Deactivate your Facebook account. If you think this is too much, you should just delete some friends you do not really talk to outside of Facebook. You should also limit Facebook usage to sharing harmless statuses and posts. As much as possible, you should avoid commenting on other people's status that could potentially create misunderstandings. You should also avoid using chat to talk to friends about important things.

In your journal

Write down the relationships you think you should end and state the reasons why. Write down the situations when you said no and explain what happened. You should also plan a solo vacation and jot down all the details in your journal, including the place you want to go, the activities you want to do, and other important details you want to experience on your trip.

Week 8—Balance Work and Play

One of the things you should have in your life is a balance of work and play. This is another important aspect of self-organization. You cannot call yourself organized if you only work hard but have no time for play or leisure. Although it is important to work hard, it is also important to find time to relax. The main reason for becoming self-organized is to be productive, be able to complete all your tasks before the deadline, and have enough free time to do the things you love.

Below is a list of tips for balancing work and play.

Take a vacation

If you think about the amount of time you spend working, you will realize that you spend a lot more time on work than on leisure. For example, you spend at least eight of your waking hours working, plus an hour or so for the commute. You spend about as much time doing things that are non-work related, but more often than not, you are too tired to exert any effort for your hobbies. You only have two days off every week, plus some holidays. This is why you should use your paid vacation instead of converting them to cash. When you take a long vacation from work, you can relax your mind and your body, which makes you more productive when you return to work.

Request for a change of schedule

You can also request for a change of schedule to balance your workload. For example, if you work as a receptionist and you receive the bulk of calls during the day, you should consider asking your supervisor to change your schedule for a few months. You can also switch shifts with a coworker just to change the pace of your work for a few weeks.

Pursue your interests

If you finish your workload on time, you will have more free time to pursue your interests and hobbies. There are a lot of people who stop doing their hobbies and pursuing their interests after they became too busy with work. You should not let this happen to you because you may feel burnt out if you only work and have no time to play. For example, if you used to love mountain climbing but stopped doing it after college and started working, you should consider starting it again. You will see how much better life is if you spend equal time working and playing.

Spend time with your family

Never choose work over your family. You may be busy with work, but you should never be too busy to spend time with your family. The main reason why you are working hard is to provide your family's basic needs like food, shelter, clothing, and education. However, your family also has emotional needs you need to fulfill. It would be ironic to not spend time with your partner and kids when they are the main reason you are working. You need to strike that balance between work and family. Create rules to ensure you do not neglect your emotional obligations to your loved ones.

For example, make it a rule to eat dinner at home no matter how big your workload may be. In addition, while you are eating dinner with your family, ignore your phone if it rings, or better yet, turn off your phone. You should also not bring unfinished work home because your time at home should be for your family. You should also attend your kids' school events and activities, and make it a point to take a vacation with them at least once a year.

Take your breaks

Sometimes, you have so much stuff to do that you end up using your break time to finish your work. You should not do this because you will start to resent doing your work. You will feel too tired and burnt out because you always work for many straight hours. Give yourself – and your mind – a break by taking the short breaks and lunch breaks that most companies offer. You can do anything you like during your break time, but do not use it for working unless you really cannot avoid it. This only becomes necessary if you fail to follow the tips provided in the previous chapters.

Aside from these breaks, you should also take a break after working straight for an hour or two. You can close your eyes, go to the rest room, drink water, and do some stretching. This very short break can help refresh your mind, and make you even more productive.

Hang out with friends

You should also spend time hanging out with friends to balance work and play. Although you were advised to say no when you do not feel like going out, you should still not forget to socialize with people you like. You should go to parties, eat out, or simply hang out at home with your buddies. Just remember to balance it all out. You should schedule your social activities after you are done with work. Also avoid going to bars and clubs every night even if you have no work to do because you will only get tired, which can affect your work and productivity.

Week 8 tasks

1. Make it a rule in your household to eat dinner as a family and to not answer phone calls at dinnertime.
2. Make a list of your forgotten hobbies and interests, and consider bringing them to back into your life. Start with buying the necessary equipment and supplies, joining a group, and reserving a time slot for your hobby in your busy schedule.
3. Finish all your work for the day or for the whole week and use the free time to do things you love. You can call a close friend and invite him over for an afternoon snack, or you can surprise your spouse by cooking dinner for your family.

In your journal

Make a list of all your activities for each day and divide them into two groups: work and play. Write the number of hours you spent for each activity and find the total. Check if the total number of hours you spent working is more than the number of hours you spent for leisure. If the former is much more than the latter, then you overworked. If leisure time is a lot more than work time, then you are not working hard enough. Find a balance between these two.

Once you do that, it means you have achieved ultimate self-organization.

Conclusion

I hope this book was able to help you learn some useful tips and tricks to achieve maximum self-organization within eight weeks.

The next step is to make sure you apply everything you learned to your personal and work life. Finishing the 8-week self-organization challenge is not the end of your journey to achieve maximum self-organization. You should continue doing the tips and tasks in this book even after completing the eight week challenge.

Thank you and good luck!

www.ingramcontent.com/pod-product-compliance
Lightning Source LLC
Chambersburg PA
CBHW070502290526
45790CB00003B/1056